"Lemonade, lemonade,"
  the bold monkey cried,
"It's only five cents,
  and it's cooling beside."
Miss Camel just sniffed
  and tossed back her head,—
"I drink only every nine days, sir,"
  she said.

Billy Goat and Nanny Goat
  went out one day to tea.
They promised Mother Goat
  they'd be good as they could be,
But on the way they passed some goats
  who cried: "Oh, see the dude!"
And then they had to go back home,
  for Billy got real rude.

Here is a Sister Piggy
  and a Brother Piggy, too,
The story they are telling here
  would not apply to you,
For selfish little sisters
  who make their brothers cry
Do not belong in houses
  but with piggies in the sty.

Mother and Father
   and little Miss Bear
Went out for a walk
   and a bit of fresh air,
Not through the dark woods
   (the old tale to repeat)
But in their best clothes,
   right down the front street.

I'm just a little puppy
   and as good as good can be,
And why they call me naughty,
   I'm sure I cannot see,
I've only carried off one shoe
   and torn the baby's hat
And chased the ducks and spilled the milk—
   there's nothing bad in that!

His manners are so charming
    and his eyes so very bright,
I do believe that we might call young Fox
    a gallant knight;
But then when he is cunning
    and just a little pert,
I'm not so sure but we should call
    this same young fox a flirt.

Beau Coyote sings a
    nightly tune
To his lady fair
    in the big, round moon.
She smiles and throws
    moonbeams to him
And he serenades
    till her light is dim.
EDITH BROWN KIRKWOOD

The Village Blacksmith

Under a spreading chestnut tree
  The village smithy stands;
The smith, a mighty man is he,
  With large and sinewy hands;
And the muscles of his brawny arms
  Are strong as iron bands.

His hair is crisp, and black, and long,
  His face is like the tan;
His brow is wet with honest sweat,
  He earns whate'er he can,
And looks the whole world in the face,
  For he owes not any man.

Week in, week out, from morn till night,
  You can hear his bellows blow;
You can hear him swing his heavy sledge,
  With measured beat and slow,
Like a sexton ringing the village bell,
  When the evening sun is low.

And children coming home from school
  Look in at the open door;
They love to see the flaming forge,
  And hear the bellows roar,
And catch the burning sparks that fly
  Like chaff from a threshing floor.

He goes on Sunday to the church,
  And sits among his boys;
He hears the parson pray and preach,
  He hears his daughter's voice,
Singing in the village choir,
  And it makes his heart rejoice.

It sounds to him like her mother's voice,
  Singing in Paradise!
He needs must think of her once more,
  How in the grave she lies;
And with his hard, rough hand he wipes
  A tear out of his eyes.

Toiling,—rejoicing,—sorrowing,
  Onward through life he goes;
Each morning sees some task begun,
  Each evening sees its close;
Something attempted, something done,
  Has earned a night's repose.

Thanks, thanks to thee, my worthy friend,
  For the lesson thou hast taught!
Thus at the flaming forge of life
  Our fortunes must be wrought;
Thus on its sounding anvil shaped
  Each burning deed and thought!

HENRY WADSWORTH LONGFELLOW

Looking Forward

When I am grown to man's estate
I shall be very proud and great,
And tell the other girls and boys
Not to meddle with my toys.
ROBERT LOUIS STEVENSON

Rain

The rain is raining all around,
It falls on field and tree,
It rains on the umbrellas here,
And on the ships at sea.
ROBERT LOUIS STEVENSON

At the Seaside

When I was down beside the sea
A wooden spade they gave to me
　To dig the sandy shore.
My holes were empty like a cup,
In every hole the sea came up,
　Till it could come no more.
ROBERT LOUIS STEVENSON

Singing

Of speckled eggs the birdie sings
　And nests among the trees;
The sailor sings of ropes and things
　In ships upon the seas.

The children sing in far Japan,
　The children sing in Spain;
The organ with the organ man
　Is singing in the rain.
ROBERT LOUIS STEVENSON

29

THE WALRUS and THE Carpenter

The sun was shining on the sea,
  Shining with all his might:
He did his very best to make
  The billows smooth and bright—
And this was odd, because it was
  The middle of the night.

The moon was shining sulkily,
  Because she thought the sun
Had got no business to be there
  After the day was done—
"It's very rude of him," she said,
  "To come and spoil the fun!"

The sea was wet as wet could be,
  The sands were dry as dry.
You could not see a cloud, because
  No cloud was in the sky:
No birds were flying overhead—
  There were no birds to fly.

The Walrus and the Carpenter
  Were walking close at hand:
They wept like anything to see
  Such quantities of sand:
"If this were only cleared away,"
  They said, "it *would* be grand!"

"If seven maids with seven mops
   Swept it for half a year,
Do you suppose," the Walrus said,
   "That they could get it clear?"
"I doubt it," said the Carpenter,
   And shed a bitter tear.

"O Oysters, come and walk with us!"
   The Walrus did beseech.
"A pleasant walk, a pleasant talk,
   Along the briny beach:
We cannot do with more than four,
   To give a hand to each."

The eldest Oyster looked at him,
   But never a word he said:
The eldest Oyster winked his eye,
   And shook his heavy head—
Meaning to say he did not choose
   To leave the oyster bed.

But four young Oysters hurried up,
   All eager for the treat:
Their coats were brushed, their faces washed,
   Their shoes were clean and neat—
And this was odd, because, you know,
   They hadn't any feet.

Four other Oysters followed them,
   And yet another four;
And thick and fast they came at last,
   And more, and more, and more—
All hopping through the frothy waves,
   And scrambling to the shore.

The Walrus and the Carpenter
   Walked on a mile or so,
And then they rested on a rock
   Conveniently low:
And all the little Oysters stood
   And waited in a row.

"The time has come," the Walrus said,
  "To talk of many things:
Of shoes—and ships—and sealing wax—
  Of cabbages—and kings—
And why the sea is boiling hot—
  And whether pigs have wings."

"But wait a bit, the Oysters cried,
  "Before we have our chat;
For some of us are out of breath,
  And all of us are fat!"
"No hurry!" said the Carpenter.
  They thanked him much for that.

"A loaf of bread," the Walrus said,
  "Is what we chiefly need:
Pepper and vinegar besides
  Are very good indeed—
Now, if you're ready, Oysters dear,
  We can begin to feed."

"But not on us!" the Oysters cried,
  Turning a little blue.
"After such kindness, that would be
  A dismal thing to do!"
"The night is fine," the Walrus said.
  "Do you admire the view?

"It was so kind of you to come!
  And you are very nice!"
The Carpenter said nothing but
  "Cut us another slice.
I wish you were not quite so deaf—
  I've had to ask you twice!"

"It seems a shame," the Walrus said,
  "To play them such a trick.
After we've brought them out so far,
  And made them trot so quick!"
The Carpenter said nothing but
  "The butter's spread too thick!"

"I weep for you," the Walrus said:
   "I deeply sympathize,"
· With sobs and tears he sorted out
   Those of the largest size,
Holding his pocket handkerchief
   Before his streaming eyes.

"O Oysters," said the Carpenter,
   "You've had a pleasant run!
Shall we be trotting home again!"
   But answer came there none—
And this was scarcely odd, because
   They'd eaten every one.

LEWIS CARROLL

34

I had a little nut tree, nothing would it bear
But a silver nutmeg and a golden pear;
The King of Spain's daughter came to visit me,
And all was because of my little nut tree.
I skipped over water, I danced over sea,
And all the birds in the air couldn't catch me.

AUTHOR UNKNOWN

The Wind

I saw you toss the kites on high
And blow the birds about the sky;
And all around I heard you pass,
Like ladies' skirts across the grass—
   O wind, a-blowing all day long,
   O wind, that sings so loud a song!

I saw the different things you did,
But always you yourself you hid.
I felt you push, I heard you call,
I could not see yourself at all—
   O wind, a-blowing all day long,
   O' wind, that sings so loud a song!

O you that are so strong and cold,
O blower, are you young or old?
Are you a beast of field and tree,
Or just a stronger child than me?
   O wind, a-blowing all day long,
   O wind, that sings so loud a song!

ROBERT LOUIS STEVENSON

A Boy's Song

Where the pools are bright and deep,
Where the gray trout lies asleep,
Up the river and o'er the lea—
That's the way for Billy and me.

Where the blackbird sings the latest,
Where the hawthorn blooms the sweetest,
Where the nestlings chirp and flee—
That's the way for Billy and me.

Where the mowers mow the cleanest,
Where the hay lies thick and greenest;
There to trace the homeward bee—
That's the way for Billy and me.

Where the hazel bank is steepest,
Where the shadow lies the deepest,
Where the clustering nuts fall free—
That's the way for Billy and me.

Why the boys should drive away
Little sweet maidens from the play,
Or love to banter and fight so well,
That's the thing I never could tell.

But this I know: I love to play,
Through the meadow, among the hay
Up the water and o'er the lea,
That's the way for Billy and me.

JAMES HOGG

Little Raindrops

Oh! where do you come from,
  You little drops of rain,
Pitter patter, pitter patter,
  Down the windowpane?

They won't let me walk
  And they won't let me play,
And they won't let me go
  Out of doors at all today.

They put away my playthings
  Because I broke them all,
And they locked up all my bricks,
  And took away my ball.

Tell me, little raindrops,
  Is that the way you play,
Pitter patter, pitter patter,
  All the rainy day?

They say I'm very naughty,
  But I've nothing else to do
But sit here at the window;
  I should like to play with you.

The little raindrops cannot speak,
  But "pitter, patter pat"
Means, "we can play on *this* side:
  Why can't you play on *that?*"
                    ANNE HAWKSHAW

♦♦♦ The Snail ♦♦♦

The frugal snail, with forecast of repose,
Carries his house with him where'er he goes;
Peeps out—and if there comes a shower of rain,
Retreats to his small domicile amain.
Touch but a tip of him, a horn,—'tis well—
He curls up in his sanctuary shell.
He's his own landlord, his own tenant; stay
Long as he will, he dreads no Quarter Day.
Himself he boards and lodges; both invites
And feasts himself; sleeps with himself o'nights.
He spares the upholsterer trouble to procure
Chattels; himself is his own furniture,
And his sole riches. Whereso'er he roam—
Knock when you will—he's sure to be at home.

CHARLES LAMB

♦♦♦ The Snake ♦♦♦

A narrow fellow in the grass
Occasionally rides;
You may have met him—did you not,
His notice sudden is.

The grass divides as with a comb,
A spotted shaft is seen;
And then it closes at your feet
And opens further on.

He likes a boggy acre,
A floor too cool for corn.
Yet when a child, and barefoot,
I more than once, at morn,

Have passed, I thought, a whiplash
Unbraiding in the sun—
When, stooping to secure it,
It wrinkled, and was gone.

Several of nature's people
I know, and they know me;
I feel for them a transport
Of cordiality;

But never met this fellow,
Attended or alone,
Without a tighter breathing,
And zero at the bone.

EMILY DICKINSON

◢◣◢ The Crocodile ◢◣◢

How doth the little crocodile
  Improve his shining tail,
And pour the waters of the Nile
  On every golden scale!

How cheerfully he seems to grin,
  How neatly spreads his claws,
And welcomes little fishes in,
  With gently smiling jaws!

LEWIS CARROLL

◢◣◢ The Bee ◢◣◢

Like trains of cars on tracks of plush
  I hear the level bee:
A jar across the flowers goes,
  Their velvet masonry

Withstands until the sweet assault
  Their chivalry consumes,
While he, victorious, tilts away
  To vanquish other blooms.

His feet are shod with gauze,
  His helmet is of gold;
His breast, a single onyx
  With chrysoprase, inlaid.

His labor is a chant,
  His idleness a tune;
Oh, for a bee's experience
  Of clovers and of noon!

EMILY DICKINSON

The Land of Counterpane

When I was sick and lay a-bed,
I had two pillows at my head,
And all my toys beside me lay
To keep me happy all the day.

And sometimes for an hour or so
I watched my leaden soldiers go,
With different uniforms and drills,
Among the bedclothes, through the hills;

And sometimes sent my ships in fleets
All up and down among the sheets;
Or brought my trees and houses out,
And planted cities all about.

I was the giant great and still
That sits upon the pillow-hill,
And sees before him, dale and plain,
The pleasant land of counterpane.

ROBERT LOUIS STEVENSON

JESSIE WILLCOX SMITH.

Seven Times One

There's no dew left on the daisies and clover,
　　There's no rain left in heaven:
I've said my "seven times" over and over,
　　Seven times one are seven.

I am old, so old, I can write a letter;
　　My birthday lessons are done;
The lambs play always, they know no better;
　　They are only one times one.

O moon! in the night I have seen you sailing
　　And shining so round and low;
You were bright! ah, bright! but your light is failing—
　　You are nothing now but a bow.

You moon, have you done something wrong in heaven
　　That God has hidden your face?
I hope if you have you will soon be forgiven,
　　And shine again in your place.

O velvet bee, you're a dusty fellow,
　　You've powdered your legs with gold!
O brave marsh marybuds, rich and yellow,
　　Give me your money to hold!

O columbine, open your folded wrapper,
　　Where two twin turtledoves dwell!
O cuckoopint, toll me the purple clapper
　　That hangs in your clear, green bell!

And show me your nest with the young ones in it;
　　I will not steal them away;
I am old! you may trust me, linnet, linnet—
　　I am seven times one today.

JEAN INGELOW

Little Things

Little drops of water,
    Little grains of sand,
Make the mighty ocean
    And the pleasant land.

Thus the little minutes,
    Humble though they be,
Make the mighty ages
    Of eternity.
EBENEZER COBHAM BREWER

To a Butterfly

I've watched you now a full half hour
Self-poised upon that yellow flower;
And, little butterfly, indeed,
I know not if you sleep or feed.

How motionless!—not frozen seas
   More motionless; and then,
What joy awaits you when the breeze
Hath found you out among the trees,
   And calls you forth again!

This plot of orchard ground is ours,
My trees they are, my sister's flowers;
Here rest your wings when they are weary,
Here lodge as in a sanctuary!

Come to us often, fear no wrong,
   Sit near us on the bough!
We'll talk of sunshine and of song,
And summer days when we were young;
Sweet childish days that were as long
   As twenty days are now.

WILLIAM WORDSWORTH

One, Two, Buckle My Shoe

One, two,
Buckle my shoe.

Three, four,
Shut the door.

Five, six,
Pick up sticks.

Seven, eight,
Lay them straight.

Nine, ten,
A good fat hen.

Eleven, twelve,
Dig and delve.

Thirteen, fourteen,
Maids a-courting.

Fifteen, sixteen,
Maids in the kitchen.

Seventeen, eighteen,
Maid in waiting.

Nineteen, twenty,
My plate is empty.

AUTHOR UNKNOWN

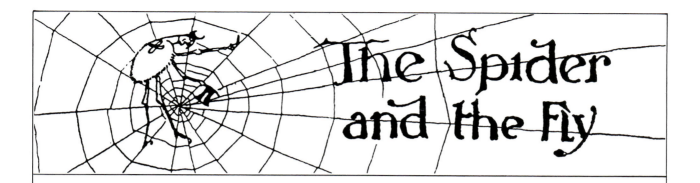

The Spider and the Fly

"Will you walk into my parlor?" said the Spider
to the Fly—
"'Tis the prettiest little parlor that ever you did
spy;
The way into my parlor is up a winding stair,
And I have many curious things to show you
when you're there."

"Oh, no, no," said the little Fly, "to ask me is
in vain,
For who goes up your winding stair can ne'er
come down again."

"I'm sure you must be weary, dear, with soaring
up so high;
Will you rest upon my little bed?" said the
Spider to the Fly.
"There are pretty curtains drawn around, the
sheets are fine and thin,
And if you like to rest a while, I'll snugly tuck
you in!"

"Oh, no, no," said the little Fly, "for I've often
heard it said,
They never, never wake again, who sleep upon
your bed!"

Said the cunning Spider to the Fly: "Dear
    friend, what can I do
To prove the warm affection I've always felt
    for you?
I have, within my pantry, good store of all that's
    nice;
I'm sure you're very welcome—will you please
    to take a slice?"

"Oh, no, no," said the little Fly; "kind sir,
    that cannot be,
I've heard what's in your pantry, and I do not
    wish to see!"

"Sweet creature," said the Spider, "you're
    witty and you're wise;
How handsome are your gauzy wings, how
    brilliant are your eyes!
I have a little looking glass upon my parlor
    shelf,
If you'll step in one moment, dear, you shall
    behold yourself."

"I thank you, gentle sir," she said, "for what
    you're pleased to say,
And bidding you good morning now, I'll call
    another day."

The Spider turned him round about, and went
    into his den,
For well he knew the silly Fly would soon come
    back again;
So he wove a subtle web, in a little corner sly,
And set his table ready, to dine upon the Fly.

Then he came out to his door again, and merrily
    did sing,—
"Come hither, hither, pretty Fly, with the pearl
    and silver wing;
Your robes are green and purple, there's a crest
    upon your head;
Your eyes are like the diamond bright, but
    mine are dull as lead!"

Alas, alas! how very soon this silly little Fly,
Hearing his wily, flattering words, came slowly
    flitting by:
With buzzing wings she hung aloft, then near
    and nearer drew,—
Thinking only of her brilliant eyes, and green
    and purple hue,
Thinking only of her crested head—poor foolish
    thing! At last,
Up jumped the cunning Spider, and fiercely
    held her fast;
He dragged her up his winding stair, into his
    dismal den,
Within his little parlor—but she ne'er came
    out again!

And now, dear little children, who may this
    story read,
To idle, silly, flattering words, I pray you ne'er
    give heed:
Unto an evil counselor close heart, and ear,
    and eye,
And take a lesson from this tale, of the Spider
    and the Fly.

MARY HOWITT

JESSIE WILLCOX SMITH.

Bed in Summer

In winter I get up at night
And dress by yellow candlelight.
In summer, quite the other way,
I have to go to bed by day.

I have to go to bed and see
The birds still hopping on the tree,
Or hear the grown-up people's feet
Still going past me in the street.

And does it not seem hard to you,
When all the sky is clear and blue,
And I should like so much to play,
To have to go to bed by day?

ROBERT LOUIS STEVENSON

The Kitten at Play

See the kitten on the wall,
Sporting with the leaves that fall,
Withered leaves, one, two, and three
Falling from the eldertree,
Through the calm and frosty air
Of the morning bright and fair.

See the kitten, how she starts,
Crouches, stretches, paws and darts
With a tiger-leap half way
Now she meets her coming prey.
Lets it go as fast and then
Has it in her power again.

Now she works with three and four,
Like an Indian conjurer;
Quick as he in feats of art,
Gracefully she plays her part;
Yet were gazing thousands there,
What would little Tabby care?

WILLIAM WORDSWORTH

The Fairy Folk

Come cuddle close in daddy's coat
  Beside the fire so bright,
And hear about the fairy folk
  That wander in the night.
For when the stars are shining clear,
  And all the world is still,
They float across the silver moon
  From hill to cloudy hill.

Their caps of red, their cloaks of green,
  Are hung with silver bells,
And when they're shaken with the wind,
  Their merry ringing swells.
And riding on the crimson moths
  With black spots on their wings,
They guide them down the purple sky
  With golden bridle rings.

They love to visit girls and boys
  To see how sweet they sleep,
To stand beside their cosy cots
  And at their faces peep.
For in the whole of fairy land
  They have no finer sight
Than little children sleeping sound
  With faces rosy bright.

On tiptoe crowding round their heads,
  When bright the moonlight beams,
They whisper little tender words
  That fill their minds with dreams;
And when they see a sunny smile,
  With lightest fingertips
They lay a hundred kisses sweet
  Upon the ruddy lips.

And then the little spotted moths
  Spread out their crimson wings,
And bear away the fairy crowd
  With shaking bridle rings.
Come, bairnies, hide in daddy's coat,
  Beside the fire so bright—
Perhaps the little fairy folk
  Will visit you tonight.

ROBERT M. BIRD

Choosing a Name

I have got a newborn sister;
I was nigh the first that kissed her.
When the nursing woman brought her
To papa, his infant daughter,
How papa's dear eyes did glisten!—
She will shortly be to christen:
And papa has made the offer,
I shall have the naming of her.
Now I wonder what would please her,
Charlotte, Julia, or Louisa?
Ann and Mary, they're too common;
Joan's too formal for a woman;
Jane's a prettier name beside;
But we had a Jane that died.
They would say, if 'twas Rebecca,
That she was a little Quaker.
Edith's pretty, but that looks
Better in old English books;
Ellen's left off long ago;
Blanche is out of fashion now.
None that I have named as yet
Are so good as Margaret.
Emily is neat and fine.
What do you think of Caroline?
How I'm puzzled and perplex'd
What to choose or think of next!
I am in a little fever
Lest the name that I shall give her
Should disgrace her or defame her;
I will leave papa to name her.

CHARLES AND MARY LAMB

60

Cupboard Land

Good night, dear toys, we love you so,
But Mother's calling, we must go;
The day has been so sweet and bright,
So go to sleep till morning light.

Good night, dear Dolly, do not fear,
For good old Dobbin's watching near,
And now and then he'll give a bray,
And that will keep the ghosts away.

Good night, dear Dobbin, stay awake
And watch o'er Dolly for my sake;
Don't let her fear—you understand,
But keep good watch in Cupboard Land.

Good night, my dear old butcher's shop,
Good night, dear drum, and flag, and top;
When day returns we'll have such fun,
Good night, good night, to everyone!

FRED E. WEATHERLY

What The Toys Do

The cupboard was closed, and the children had gone,
There were only the stars in the sky looking on;
When up jumped the toys and peeped out on the sky,
For they always awake—when there's nobody by.

The children were far away saying their prayers,
So the toys lightly stole down the shadowy stairs,
And each said to each, "We'll be off, you and I,"
For the toys—they can speak,—when there's nobody by.

So off to the city they went, two and two,
To see if, perchance, any good they could do,
To cheer the poor children whose lives are so sad,
For the toys always try to make everyone glad.

FRED E. WEATHERLY

Where did you come from, baby dear?
"Out of the everywhere into here."

Where did you get those eyes so blue?
"Out of the sky as I came through."

What makes the light in them sparkle and spin?
"Some of the starry spikes left in."

Where did you get that little tear?
"I found it waiting when I got here."

What makes your forehead so smooth and high?
"A soft hand stroked it as I went by."

What makes your cheek like a warm white rose?
"I saw something better than anyone knows."

Whence that three-cornered smile of bliss?
"Three angels gave me at once a kiss."

Where did you get this pearly ear?
"God spoke, and it came out to hear."

Where did you get those arms and hands?
"Love made itself into bonds and bands."

AUTHOR UNKNOWN

♦♦♦ The Blind Men and the Elephant ♦♦♦

It was six men of Indostan
 To learning much inclined,
Who went to see the elephant
 (Though all of them were blind),
That each by observation
 Might satisfy his mind.

The First approached the elephant,
 And, happening to fall
Against his broad and sturdy side,
 At once began to bawl:
"God bless me! but the elephant
 Is nothing but a wall!"

The Second, feeling of the tusk,
  Cried: "Ho! what have we here
So very round and smooth and sharp?
  To me 'tis mighty clear
This wonder of an elephant
  Is very like a spear!"

The Third approached the animal,
  And, happening to take
The squirming trunk within his hands,
  Thus boldly up and spake:
"I see," quoth he, "the elephant
  Is very like a snake!"

The Fourth reached out his eager hand,
  And felt about the knee:
"What most this wondrous beast is like
  Is mighty plain," quoth he;
"'Tis clear enough the elephant
  Is very like a tree."

The Fifth, who chanced to touch the ear,
  Said: "E'en the blindest man
Can tell what this resembles most;
  Deny the fact who can,
This marvel of an elephant
  Is very like a fan!"

The Sixth no sooner had begun
  About the beast to grope,
Than, seizing on the swinging tail
  That fell within his scope,
"I see," quoth he, "the elephant
  Is very like a rope!"

And so these men of Indostan
  Disputed loud and long,
Each in his own opinion
  Exceeding stiff and strong,
Though each was partly in the right,
  And all were in the wrong!

So, oft in theologic wars
  The disputants, I ween,
Rail on in utter ignorance
  Of what each other mean,
And prate about an elephant
  Not one of them has seen!
                    JOHN GODFREY SAXE

Sea Fever

I must go down to the seas again, to the lonely sea and the sky,
And all I ask is a tall ship and a star to steer her by;
And the wheel's kick and the wind's song and the white sail's shaking,
And a gray mist on the sea's face, and a gray dawn breaking.

I must go down to the seas again, for the call of the running tide
Is a wild call and a clear call that may not be denied;
And all I ask is a windy day with the white clouds flying,
And the flung spray and the blown spume, and the sea gulls crying.

I must go down to the seas again, to the vagrant gypsy life,
To the gull's way and the whale's way where the wind's like a whetted knife;
And all I ask is a merry yarn from a laughing fellow-rover,
And quiet sleep and a sweet dream when the long trick's over.

JOHN MASEFIELD

THE SWING.

How do you like to go up in a swing,
  Up in the air so blue?
Oh, I do think it the pleasantest thing
  Ever a child can do!

Up in the air and over the wall,
  Till I can see so wide,
Rivers and trees and cattle and all
  Over the countryside—

Till I look down on the garden green,
  Down on the roof so brown—
Up in the air I go flying again,
  Up in the air and down!

ROBERT LOUIS STEVENSON

My Little Sister

I have a little sister,
   She is only two years old;
But to us at home, who love her,
   She is worth her weight in gold.

We often play together;
   And I begin to find,
That to make my sister happy,
   I must be very kind;

And always very gentle
   When we run about and play,
Nor ever take her playthings
   Or little toys away.

I must not vex or tease her,
   Nor ever angry be
With the darling little sister
   That God has given me.

AUTHOR UNKNOWN

JESSIE WILLCOX SMITH

When the Wind
Is in the East

When the wind is in the East,
'Tis neither good for man nor beast;
When the wind is in the North,
The skillful fisher goes not forth;
When the wind is in the South,
It blows the bait in the fishes' mouth;
When the wind is in the West,
Then 'tis at the very best.

AUTHOR UNKNOWN

Come When You Are Called

Where's Susan, and Kitty, and Jane?
Where's Billy, and Sammy, and Jack?
O! there they are, down in the lane,
Go, Betty, and bring them all back.

But Billy is rude and won't come,
And Sammy is running too fast;
Come, dear little children, come home,
And Billy is coming at last.

I'm glad he remembers what's right,
For though he likes sliding on ice,
He should not be long out of sight,
And never want sending for twice.

AUTHOR UNKNOWN

Twinkle, Twinkle,
Little Star

Twinkle, twinkle, little star,
How I wonder what you are!
Up above the world so high
Like a diamond in the sky.

When the blazing sun is gone,
When he nothing shines upon,
Then you show your little light,
Twinkle, twinkle, all the night.

Then the traveler in the dark
Thanks you for your tiny spark!
He could not see which way to go,
If you did not twinkle so.

In the dark blue sky you keep,
And often through my curtains peep,
For you never shut your eye
Till the sun is in the sky.

As your bright and tiny spark
Lights the traveler in the dark,
Though I know not what you are,
Twinkle, twinkle, little star.

JANE TAYLOR

♦♦♦ The Mock Turtle's Song ♦♦♦

"Will you walk a little faster?" said a whiting to a snail,
"There's a porpoise close behind us, and he's treading on my tail.
See how eagerly the lobsters and the turtles all advance!
They are waiting on the shingle—will you come and join the dance?
Will you, won't you, will you, won't you, will you join the dance?
Will you, won't you, will you, won't you, won't you join the dance?

"You can really have no notion how delightful it will be,
When they take us up and throw us, with the lobsters, out to sea!"
But the snail replied, "Too far, too far!" and gave a look askance—
Said he thanked the whiting kindly, but he would not join the dance.
Would not, could not, would not, could not, would not join the dance.
Would not, could not, would not, could not, could not join the dance.

"What matters it how far we go?" his scaly friend replied,
"There is another shore, you know, upon the other side.
The further off from England the nearer is to France—
Then turn not pale, beloved snail, but come and join the dance.
Will you, won't you, will you, won't you, will you join the dance?
Will you, won't you, will you, won't you, won't you join the dance?"

LEWIS CARROLL

Jabberwocky

'Twas brillig, and the slithy toves
    Did gyre and gimble in the wabe;
All mimsy were the borogoves,
    And the mome raths outgrabe.

"Beware the Jabberwock, my son!
    The jaws that bite, the claws that catch!
Beware the Jubjub bird, and shun
    The frumious Bandersnatch!"

He took his vorpal sword in hand:
    Long time the manxome foe he sought.—
So rested he by the Tumtum tree,
    And stood awhile in thought.

And as in uffish thought he stood,
    The Jabberwock, with eyes of flame,
Came whiffling through the tulgey wood,
    And burbled as it came!

One, two! One, two! And through and through
    The vorpal blade went snicker-snack!
He left it dead, and with its head
    He went galumphing back.

"And hast thou slain the Jabberwock?
    Come to my arms, my beamish boy!
O frabjous day! Callooh! Callay!"
    He chortled in his joy.

'Twas brillig, and the slithy toves
    Did gyre and gimble in the wabe;
All mimsy were the borogoves,
    And the mome raths outgrabe.

LEWIS CARROLL

Lullaby

Sweet and low, sweet and low,
  Wind of the western sea,
Low, low, breathe and blow,
  Wind of the western sea!

Over the rolling waters go,
Come from the dying moon and blow,
  Blow him again to me;
While my little one, while my pretty one,
    sleeps.

Sleep and rest, sleep and rest,
  Father will come to thee soon;
Rest, rest, on mother's breast,
  Father will come to thee soon;

Father will come to his babe in the nest,
Silver sails all out of the west
  Under the silver moon:
Sleep, my little one; sleep, my pretty one,
    sleep.

ALFRED, LORD TENNYSON

The Butterfly's Ball

"Come, take up your hats, and away let us haste
To the Butterfly's Ball and the Grasshopper's Feast;
The trumpeter, Gadfly, has summoned the crew,
And the revels are now only waiting for you."

So said little Robert, and pacing along,
His merry companions came forth in a throng,
And on the smooth grass by the side of a wood,
Beneath a broad oak that for ages has stood,
Saw the children of earth and the tenants of air
For an evening's amusement together repair.

And there came the Beetle, so blind and so black,
Who carried the Emmet, his friend, on his back;
And there was the Gnat and the Dragonfly too,
With all their relations, green, orange, and blue.

And there came the Moth, with his plumage of down,
And the Hornet, in jacket of yellow and brown,
Who with him the Wasp, his companion, did bring:
They promised that evening to lay by their sting.

And the sly little Dormouse crept out of his hole,
And brought to the Feast his blind brother, the Mole.
And the Snail, with his horns peeping out of his shell,
Came from a great distance—the length of an ell.

A mushroom their table, and on it was laid
A water-dock leaf, which a tablecloth made.
The viands were various, to each of their taste,
And the Bee brought her honey to crown the repast.

Then close on his haunches, so solemn and wise,
The Frog from a corner looked up to the skies;
And the Squirrel, well-pleased such diversions to see,
Mounted high overhead and looked down from a tree.

Then out came a Spider, with fingers so fine,
To show his dexterity on the tight line.
From one branch to another his cobwebs he slung,
Then quick as an arrow he darted along.

But just in the middle—oh! shocking to tell,
From his rope, in an instant, poor Harlequin fell.
Yet he touched not the ground, but with talons outspread,
Hung suspended in air, at the end of a thread.

Then the Grasshopper came, with a jerk and a spring,
Very long was his leg, though but short was his wing;
He took but three leaps, and was soon out of sight,
Then chirped his own praises the rest of the night.

With step so majestic, the Snail did advance,
And promised the gazers a minuet to dance:
But they all laughed so loud that he pulled in his head,
And went to his own little chamber to bed.
Then as evening gave way to the shadows of night,
Their watchman, the Glow-worm, came out with a light.

"Then home let us hasten while yet we can see,
For no watchman is waiting for you and for me."
So said little Robert, and pacing along,
His merry companions returned in a throng.

WILLIAM ROSCOE

Wynken, Blynken, and Nod.

Wynken, Blynken, and Nod one night
   Sailed off in a wooden shoe—
Sailed on a river of crystal light,
   Into a sea of dew.
"Where are you going, and what do you wish?"
   The old moon asked the three.
"We have come to fish for the herring-fish
   That live in this beautiful sea;
Nets of silver and gold have we!"
    Said Wynken, Blynken, and Nod.

The old moon laughed and sang a song,
   As they rocked in the wooden shoe,
And the wind that sped them all night long,
   Ruffled the waves of dew.

The little stars were the herring-fish
    That lived in that beautiful sea—
"Now cast your nets wherever you wish—
    But never afeard are we";
So cried the stars to the fishermen three:
    Wynken, Blynken, and Nod.

All night long their nets they threw
    For the fish in the twinkling foam—
Then down from the sky came the wooden shoe,
    Bringing the fishermen home;
'Twas all so pretty a sail, it seemed
    As if it could not be;
And some folks thought 'twas a dream they'd dreamed
    Of sailing that beautiful sea—
But I shall name you the fishermen three:
    Wynken, Blynken, and Nod.

Wynken and Blynken are two little eyes,
  And Nod is a little head,
And the wooden shoe that sailed the skies
  Is a wee one's trundle bed.
So shut your eyes while mother sings
  Of wonderful sights that be,
And you shall see the beautiful things
  As you rock in the misty sea,
Where the old shoe rocked the fishermen three:
  Wynken, Blynken, and Nod.

                              EUGENE FIELD

The Land of Nod

From breakfast on through all the day
At home among my friends I stay;
But every night I go abroad
Afar into the Land of Nod.

All by myself I have to go,
With none to tell me what to do—
All alone beside the streams
And up the mountainsides of dreams.

The strangest things are there for me,
Both things to eat and things to see,
And many frightening sights abroad
Till morning in the Land of Nod.

Try as I like to find the way,
I never can get back by day,
Nor can remember plain and clear
The curious music that I hear.

ROBERT LOUIS STEVENSON

Good Night

Little baby, lay your head
On your pretty cradle bed;
Shut your eye-peeps, now the day
And the light are gone away;
All the clothes are tucked in tight;
Little baby dear, good night.

Yes, my darling, well I know
How the bitter wind doth blow;
And the winter's snow and rain
Patter on the windowpane:
But they cannot come in here,
To my little baby dear;

For the window shutteth fast,
Till the stormy night is past;
And the curtains warm are spread
Round about her cradle bed:
So till morning shineth bright,
Little baby dear, good night.

JANE TAYLOR

88

Index of Poets